D0128364

# HOUSE
## THE HYBRID
### Designing with Sun, Wind, Water, and Earth

Catherine Wanek

**GIBBS SMITH**
TO ENRICH AND INSPIRE HUMANKIND

First Edition
14 13 12 11 10     5 4 3 2 1

Published by
Gibbs Smith
P.O. Box 667
Layton, Utah 84041

1.800.835.4993 orders
www.gibbs-smith.com

Designed by Debra McQuiston
Printed and bound in China
Gibbs Smith books are printed on either recycled,
100 percent post-consumer waste, FSC-certified
papers or on paper produced from a 100 percent
certified sustainable forest/controlled wood source.

Library of Congress Cataloging-in-Publication Data

Wanek, Catherine.
 The hybrid house : designing with sun, wind,
water, and earth / Catherine Wanek. -- 1st ed.
   p. cm.
 ISBN-13: 978-1-4236-0316-0
 ISBN-10: 1-4236-0316-8
 1. Architecture, Domestic—Environmental
aspects. 2. Architecture and energy conservation.
3. Architecture—Environmental aspects. I. Title.
 NA7117.3.W36 2010
 690'.8047—dc22
                                    2009034983

I am most grateful to the many designers and building professionals represented in this book who have inspired me with their projects, and freely offered their knowledge and experience, especially architects Kelly Lerner, Werner Schmidt, Margareta Schwartz, Paula Baker-Laporte, and Bill Hutchins.

Numerous other great minds have contributed to my understanding of how buildings work, including architects and engineers Bruce King, David Eisenberg, David Arkin, Dan Smith, Dirk Scharmer, John Straube, and Matthias Boenisch, and inspired builders Athena and Bill Steen, Barbara Jones and Bee Rowan, Chris Magwood, Chris Prelitz, Derek Roff, Mark Piepkorn, Paul Koppana, Kaki Hunter, Doni Kiffmeyer, Ianto Evans, Fleming Abrahamson, Steen Moller, Lars Keller, Herbert Gruber, and Andre De Bouter.

At Gibbs Smith, I'm especially grateful for the encouragement of my editor, Michelle Witte, the trusting support of Christopher Robbins, Madge Baird, and Suzanne Taylor; and the beautiful book design by Debra McQuiston. Editorial input from my good friend and author Marsha Scarbrough benefited the manuscript significantly.

My husband, Pete Fust, deserves my deepest appreciation for keeping the home fires burning during the many trips to gather material for this book. Thanks also to my mother, Betty Wanek, often my traveling companion, for wholeheartedly embracing my agenda and being interested in everything.

This book is dedicated to the homeowners I have visited, for being modern-day pioneers on the journey to a conscious lifestyle. Many more than are represented in this book have shared their houses, passions and dreams with me, and often a spare bed and home-cooked meal as well. Thank you all, and namaste.

conten

# what is
# a hybrid
# house?

In the last decade, hybrid cars have increased transport fuel efficiency dramatically. By harnessing overlooked energy sources inherent in auto technology and combining energy systems, a hybrid engine reduces fossil fuel consumption without sacrificing performance. In a similar way, hybrid houses reduce outside energy requirements with smart design, energy-saving construction techniques, and home-generated power.

A hybrid house is not a cookie-cutter floor plan, kit-home, or pre-fab module. Rather, it is a design that relates and responds to its climate and location. As the name implies, a hybrid house is a thoughtful combination of construction materials and methods, selected for resource and energy efficiency. A hybrid design also harvests natural energy flows and is integrated with the landscape around it.

Similar energy-saving construction concepts might be called a "Passivhaus" in Germany and Austria, an "Autark" home in Switzerland, or a "Zero Net Energy home" in U.S. green-building circles.

However, while energy conservation is a key consideration, a hybrid house must not be a toxic box. Rather, it is constructed with materials that are healthful for the residents, who will typically spend 65 percent of their lives inside their homes. Benign materials also ensure that the house will not become a hazardous dump when the building's life comes to an end.

The "embodied energy" and life cycle of materials must also be considered in the energy equation. Choosing local materials reduces transportation costs and $CO_2$, durable materials last longer and require less maintenance, and less-processed natural materials will decompose harmlessly back into the earth. This "cradle-to-cradle" approach is by definition the most sustainable way to approach building design and construction.

# dangers and
# opportunities

Many scientists believe that the ecology of Planet Earth is at a tipping point. The consensus is that global warming, due to increased carbon in the atmosphere, is causing changes in climates around the globe. Humans are probably the main cause of these atmospheric conditions, and it's up to us to reverse the trend before it's too late.

The fastest and easiest way to lower our "carbon footprint" is to reduce energy consumption through conservation. Interestingly, the energy required to operate buildings, along with the embodied energy of construction materials, show buildings to be the largest energy-consuming and greenhouse-gas-emitting sector of the U.S. economy. Since buildings account for half of all the energy we use, mostly for heating and cooling, the best place to start is right here at home. The good news is that we don't really need to give things up if we target the energy that we currently waste.

By increasing the energy efficiency of our homes, we can reduce consumption without sacrificing comfort. The knowledge and technology already exist. Government-funded projects in the 1980s demonstrated that no-cost design changes can reduce the energy use in a home by 50 percent, and that additional insulation creates immediate and ongoing energy savings. According to calculations by Architecture 2030, this kind of conservation by itself could add up to reductions in greenhouse gas emissions sufficient to limit global warming to a manageable level.

Clearly, any solution to global warming must involve the design and construction of our buildings. If architects, builders, developers, and homeowners (encouraged by laws, incentives, and common sense) improve energy efficiency in all new construction and remodeling projects over the next two decades, the cumulative effect could turn our planet back from a climate in crisis, and onto a path towards true sustainability.

Moreover, if those of us living in industrialized nations begin choosing more energy-efficient, healthful, "hybrid" houses, we create replicable models for developing countries. And even as our planet's population rises, sustainable building practices offer the opportunity of comfortable, affordable housing across the globe.

For instance, at the same time America's farmers are growing grain for bread, beer, and sushi, they are growing potential building materials. Straw and rice hulls are by-products of food production that offer great value as insulation. Each year U.S. farmers produce 200 million tons of straw alone—ten times more than would be needed to insulate every new home that is built each year in America. Utilizing agricultural "waste" as a building material is one of many sustainable strategies applicable anywhere in the world.

## The Bottom Line

A hybrid house may not be the cheapest home on the block, but any additional building costs will be recouped many times over by the long-term savings in operating energy. Plus, energy-saving designs allow architects to reduce the size of, and even eliminate, heating and cooling systems. So investing in quality construction can actually save money and minimize environmental impact, while maintaining all the comforts of home.

Perhaps even greater comfort is the peace of mind in knowing that a hybrid house is a healthy house. In the same way that junk food is bad to ingest, junk construction is harmful to live inside. Replacing toxic building materials with natural materials is far better for the planet, and for people, too. After all, how much is your health worth?

Choices and decisions made while new buildings are designed and built will have long-lasting effects. An energy-efficient, healthy home, office, store, or factory not only benefits the initial owner but also future generations. Put in economic terms, sustainability means treating the earth as an investment: using the dividends and interest provided by nature, without depleting the capital.

The "hybrid houses" ahead are contemporary examples of designers, builders, and homeowners facing the challenge of achieving close-to-zero energy consumption while still living a great twenty-first-century life. The choices of these homeowners reflect specific climates,

available resources, and personal aesthetics. When these healthful, energy-saving, cradle-to-cradle systems are optimized, the necessary process of housing ourselves can become a step toward a sustainable lifestyle.

**Sustainable Development:** "That which meets the needs of the present without compromising the ability of future generations to meet their own needs. Sustainability is a method of harvesting or using a resource so that the resource is not depleted or permanently damaged."
—U.N. World Commission on Environment and Development

**Green Buildings** "promote resource conservation, including energy efficiency, renewable energy and water conservation, minimize waste, create a healthful and comfortable environment. The entire life cycle of the building and its components is considered as well as the economic and environmental impact and performance."
—U.S. Department of Energy (DOE)

**Resilience:** "The ability of natural or human systems to survive in the face of great change. To be resilient, a system must be able to adapt to changing circumstances and develop new ways to thrive. Ecologically, resilience describes the ability of natural systems to return to equilibrium after adapting to changes."
—World Watch Institute (www.worldwatch.org)

**Cradle-to-Cradle:** "An approach to construction and manufacturing that emulates the intelligence of natural systems. "Cradle to cradle" products can be used, recycled, and used again without losing any material quality, virtually eliminating the concept of waste. A commercially productive, socially beneficial, and ecologically intelligent approach to the making of things."
—William McDonough and Michael Braungart (www.mcdonough.com)

stra

**tegies**

Reducing consumption is the quickest way to begin reversing the trend and start becoming a "carbon neutral" society. Both society and consumers benefit from conservation by saving the cost of energy not consumed. Doesn't that mean we have to give up things? Not necessarily. We can begin by reducing the amount of things we waste.

# design
# strategies
## for sustainability

A hybrid house design strives to create a comfortable and healthy living space with the minimum of resources, pollution, and energy. Fossil fuel use is reduced through solar orientation and material selection, and by incorporating natural cooling, ventilation, and daylighting strategies. Residents can further reduce power consumption by selecting efficient appliances and developing conservative habits to eliminate plain old waste.

In a typical conventionally built house, space heating and cooling consume more than 50 percent of the total energy used by residents. A hybrid house lessens these energy needs with a super-insulated "building envelope," which acts like a thermos bottle to keep a home either warm or cool, depending on the season.

With efficiency reducing demand, the additional modest amount of energy homeowners will then need to maintain comfort and operate equipment can be supplied by renewable sources such as solar electric systems (photovoltaics), solar hot water heating, wind, and other low-carbon sources.

## Harvesting On-site Energy

Solar energy drives our planet. Direct sunlight changes to heat as it strikes a surface. Collecting this energy is called "passive" solar heating because no motors, fans, or pumps are involved.

Passive solar design takes advantage of the seasonal arc of the sun, which is overhead in the sky in mid-summer and drops to a lower arc to the south in the winter (in the Northern Hemisphere). South-facing glass lets the winter sun's heat into a house through windows, sunspaces, and Trombe walls. Roof overhangs are calculated to shade south windows in the warmer seasons.

East and west windows allow in light and heat too. Since in summer too much sunlight can overheat a space, good design strives for a balance of heating and shading for each climate and site. On the north side of the house, windows and doors are typically minimized.

Thermal windows will pay for themselves in insulation value, air tightness, and durability. To enhance good windows, it's important to install insulating curtains or shades to prevent heat loss at night. And, finally, passive solar design requires active owners: people who understand when to open and close their windows and curtains for comfort and energy conservation.

## An Airtight Insulated Envelope

Once the sun has warmed the house through the windows, a well-insulated, airtight building envelope retains the heat. Insulation materials resist the flow of heat energy, isolating the inside of a building from the temperatures outside. Measured in "R-value" per inch, it is the small pockets of sealed air in foams, fiberglass, and straw bales that make them effective insulators.

Incorporating walls and ceilings full of insulation in a building is like adding a down comforter to your bed. It's important to insulate foundations, too. Seal all penetrations against air infiltration, and you create a space that is easy to heat and to cool.

ABOVE: Inside a super-insulated building envelope, residents can achieve heating comfort almost entirely from the sun, even here in the Swiss Alps. Too much sun? Flip a switch and motorized exterior shades descend, controlling the amount of solar heat allowed inside.

BELOW: On the north and west, windows are minimized to reduce heat loss and heat gain.

# In a building, the insulated envelope is compromised around doors, windows, and ceiling penetrations:

Areas where air can leak through minor imperfections. Also, "thermal bridging" will impact efficiency. This effect is common in stick-frame buildings, where the structural studs span the wall. Since the R-value of a wooden 2 x 6 is less than the insulated wall cavity, cold will creep in around and through the studs.

## Mass for Thermal Storage

There are two parts to solar comfort—how much heat or cool you can capture and how much you can store. "Thermal mass" materials act like a battery, storing heat and stabilizing temperatures inside a building. The more sun there is shining in, the more mass is needed to absorb it so your home won't overheat.

Mass materials are heavy and dense, like stone, bricks, adobe blocks, and concrete. These materials absorb the temperature of the air around them, in addition to heating up as the sun shines on them. When the air around them starts to cool, they release their stored heat. Incorporated inside a well-insulated building envelope, mass materials will stabilize the day-to-night swings in temperature. During both winter and summer, thermal mass will keep a home more comfortable with less energy use than a home of lightweight materials, such as frame walls and wooden floors.

## Natural Cooling Strategies

Most heat gain and loss is through the roof, so insulation above the ceiling works for keeping cool, too. Also, a light-colored reflective roof will deflect significant heat energy. A radiant barrier located just below the roofing material adds even more deflection of heat energy—so in a warm sunny climate a radiant barrier is worth installing.

Ventilation is a natural strategy for free cooling. Double-hung windows on both sides of the house in the path of the prevailing wind allow fresh air into a home while exhausting the interior air out the other side. Since hot air rises, open an upstairs window if you have one. A whole-house fan that exhausts warm air through the attic is particularly effective, at a fraction of the energy cost of air conditioning.

During the summer, ventilation is especially effective at night, when outside temperatures

▲●■ Inside a building, mass materials stabilize temperatures, helping to create a comfortable living space.

South-facing windows harvest light and heat, while providing views and allowing for ventilation. In the winter they also lose heat after the sun goes down, so choose window size and placement according to your climate and building site.

During the summer, the micro-climate created by a mature treescape helps keep the neighborhood cool. Deciduous trees lose their leaves in the fall, allowing a home to harvest solar energy during colder weather. In addition to the direct benefits to people, a lush landscape provides animal habitat, prevents erosion, and sequesters carbon.

typically drop. Capturing the cool night air, absorbing and storing the coolness inside mass materials, then shutting windows and doors in the morning when it begins warming up outside, can work to keep a home comfortable all day without mechanical cooling.

Creating shade also helps a building keep its cool. An over-hanging roof on the south and a covered porch on the west keep sunshine from striking and heating up the exterior walls. And here's where a beautiful treescape can save you money, cooling the micro-climate around your house by shading it from the sun, and by transpiring moisture into the air.

Heating water is a very efficient way to harvest solar energy. Domestic solar thermal heaters are the second most cost-effective technology to install, after a solar clothes dryer (a clothesline). Water is the ultimate thermal mass material. It can store nearly twice the heat energy as concrete or earth blocks. Around the world, many different systems have been invented to effectively collect solar energy to heat water.

# In temperate climates the sun may be seasonal.

Solar electric panels and wind turbines generate electricity close to home. Tying local, renewable sources of energy to "the grid" reduces line loss and the risk of widespread system failure, and can reduce domestic energy bills to insignificance.

Typically, solar systems depend on temperature sensors, valves, electronic switches, antifreeze, and/or heat exchangers to keep pipes from freezing in the winter. However, the most practical solar hot water heaters are often the simplest.

In some climates, a solar thermal system can provide all the hot water a hybrid household needs, for both domestic use and space heating. A radiant heating system circulates warm water (about 100 degrees Fahrenheit) through durable polyethylene (PEX) tubing encased in concrete floors or thick plaster. As it is pumped through the system, the warm water radiates its heat into the mass surrounding it. When the sun is shining, a solar system can furnish this heat,

backed up by a conventional or on-demand hot water heater.

With heat stored in the mass of the floor or walls, air exchange can occur in a home without causing discomfort. In fact, radiant heat is widely preferred over systems that circulate hot air. Moreover, conventional forced-air distribution ducts commonly leak as much as 30 percent of their precious cargo. While radiant heating systems have a reputation for being expensive to install, their efficiency and pay-back from energy savings make them quite cost effective in most climates.

Clean water is becoming increasingly precious, both for household and farmland use. One obvious solution is integrating systems in our homes that use water multiple times. Simply reusing gray water (shower and sinks) to flush toilets could reduce domestic water consumption by 40 percent! Or the adventurous homeowner might install a composting toilet and plumb the gray water outlet so that it waters the landscape.

Harvesting rainwater from the roof is another strategy for watering the garden and flushing toilets. In some regions with brackish groundwater, rain is the main source of water for all household use. Citizens of those localities already realize how precious clean water is and they have integrated conservation and multi-tasking into their daily lives.

It is unsustainable to pollute our drinking water, but this is exactly what we do when we flush a toilet. In municipalities, human "waste" goes to huge energy-intensive treatment plants. Yet, on both a household and community level, biological systems have been developed to harmlessly process human waste into food for bacteria and plants. It's time our society learned to close the loop on organic waste and recognize the significant nutrient value it offers.

# Choosing
# **Building**
## Materials

When selecting from the smorgasbord of building systems and materials, a designer must make informed decisions, and weigh benefits and budget. To create a beautiful, healthful living space with minimal energy use, very often the most ecological choices are traditional natural materials. These can also be the most cost-effective choices.

## Why choose natural materials?

As renewable resources, natural materials can be sustainably harvested. Because they are minimally processed, they are unlikely to contain toxic chemical components. Also, less processing means that the building materials are typically inexpensive, and if acquired locally, they will require the least transportation energy to deliver. In fact, natural materials can sometimes be harvested for free, right on the building site, like that tree growing in the middle of the house, and the sub-soil dug up from the foundation.

Curb appeal need not be sacrificed for ecological efficiency. A home built with natural materials can achieve nearly any architectural look desired, and can fit into any neighborhood. In fact, there's no limit to the creative combinations of traditional and contemporary materials and methodologies that can be incorporated into a hybrid house design.

## A Healthful Home

The goal of creating a healthy home can't be overstated, since average Americans spend more than 90 percent of their time in buildings. Indoor air quality is affected by products that we build with and bring into our houses. Probably the most important strategy for benign living space is to build and furnish our homes with non-toxic materials.

By building with many conventional materials, we are actually creating our living space with potentially harmful substances. Highly processed construction materials including manufactured lumber, composite woods, fiberglass insulation, carpet padding, paints, stains, and cleaning products, contain toxic chemicals—such as formaldehyde and volatile organic compounds (VOCs)—that can negatively impact human health.

A hybrid house may not eliminate all toxic materials, but it minimizes their use, replacing them with less-processed natural materials wherever possible: real wood instead of composites, and natural insulation rather than fiberglass or foams.

Traditional earthen plasters have begun to be recognized for their beneficial qualities of balancing excess humidity and helping to purify the air. Clay plasters can actually absorb toxins from the air, like ceramic filters help purify water and clay facials remove impurities from skin.

For good indoor air quality, try not to build with or bring toxic materials into your healthy home. Ask questions and read labels. Let your nose guide you—the sniff test can often tip you off to fumes from carpet, furniture, and cleaning chemicals that disagree with you. You can go nuts trying to be a purist about this or tolerate a modicum of impurity. Take your cue from how you and your family feel.

## Fungus among Us

Mold is the asbestos of our time. It can cause flu-like symptoms, and a serious case of certain

a hybrid house
minimizes mechanical complexity
in favor of more simple
technology for low energy use,
maintenance and reliability.

Construction and demolition debris accounts for up to 30 percent of the waste stream flowing to urban landfills.

molds can even be fatal. If unchecked, mold can completely ruin a house and its furnishings. It's popping up in so many more places that insurance companies have started excluding it from home-owner's coverage. Mold spores are everywhere, but a mold invasion is preventable by eliminating the conditions that allow it to thrive.

Essentially, mold is a moisture problem. The roof or plumbing could be leaking. Moisture could also be seeping through walls in the basement. All organic materials can be food for mold, including wood products, particle board, fiber boards, the paper backing on gypsum board, straw bales, car-peting and rugs, and so on. Sunlight kills mold, and so do chemicals like bleach and hydrogen peroxide. Also, traditional lime plaster is naturally antifungal and antibiotic, so it is an appropriate finish for bathrooms and kitchens.

Forced-air HVAC systems are common because they incorporate heating, cooling and air exchange all in a single unit. But in terms of comfort and energy efficiency, radiant heating systems are superior, without the potential for harboring mold. It might be a better choice to forgo an HVAC system, and to have separate strategies for heating, cooling and ventilation.

## A Low-Carbon Life Cycle

The Life-Cycle Assessment is a cradle-to-grave approach that tracks the environmental impact of products from raw material extraction through eventual disposal or recycling. Life cycle considerations include size, site impact, durability, renewable resources, embodied energy, and energy efficiency.

The longer your home lasts, the longer the period of time its construction costs and environmental effects will be spread out, or amortized. Choose materials that will require minimum maintenance and that are reusable and recyclable. A classic design that is accessible, flexible, and durable will be the most likely to be cared for by the humans it will serve, thereby ensuring a long lifespan.

## Renewable Resources

Eighty percent of the homes in North America are built using conventional "platform framing," or "stick frame" construction. An average 2 x 6 wood-frame structural system requires lumber and wood products from approximately forty full-grown trees, which is the equivalent of clear-cutting two acres of mature forest. These trees will take a minimum of thirty years to grow back.

An estimated 30 percent can be saved through reduction, recycling, and material substitution.

It bears mentioning that conventional "forced-air" heating, ventilation, and air conditioning (HVAC) systems that deliver warm or cool air throughout a house, can themselves be a source of allergens and mold. Moisture condensing inside the system can create a good environment for mold growth, and, when engaged by the thermostat, these systems begin blowing dust, and whatever else is in there, right into the living spaces.

"Advanced framing" techniques, truss systems, and I-joist systems all use less wood while achieving the same structural strength. A traditional timber-frame structure also uses mature trees, but its careful design reduces overall wood use by one-third to one-half, and the structure can literally last for centuries.

The deconstruction of existing buildings such as old barns, factories, and schools allows for salvaging lumber that is often of higher quality than today's freshly milled wood. Linoleum, ceramic tile, and stone can be used for flooring and countertops, and recycled plastic "wood" can replace real wood in decking and outdoor furniture. Interior doors are now typically made from pressed wood composites, though beware of toxic construction adhesives.

Forest Stewardship Council certifies companies that demonstrate sustainable harvesting techniques. It has a rigorous set of criteria for managing forest lands and scrutinizes forest management practices. While it adds to the cost, certified wood substitutes directly for conventional dimensional lumber. It can be framing lumber, decking, or panel products, such as plywood and OSB.

Harvesting resources in a sustainable way is made easier by selecting materials that are not depleted but renewed regularly by nature. Grown annually, a crop of grain such as wheat, rice, oats, barley, rye, flax, etc., leaves a dry stem of straw when harvested that is considered an agricultural waste. Gathered into bales, straw has great potential in building systems to take some pressure off of timber resources. Stacked into walls and plastered, it is a durable insulating material that can also be used structurally.

Straw and rice hulls can also be compressed into strong panels that can stand alone (without studs) as interior walls. Straw board and rice board can also substitute for particleboard in carpet underlayment, cabinet carcasses, and shelves. Most straw board uses adhesive that doesn't contain formaldehyde.

## Embodied Energy

Some modern building materials require so much energy to produce and transport that their "carbon footprint" is enormous. Steel, aluminum, and cement are in this category. Foam insulations are also energy-intensive and, for the most part, are produced from petroleum. So, while these are all very common and useful materials in construction, their "embodied energy" makes these materials very precious, in terms of their planetary impact.

Embodied energy equals earth extraction, processing, and transportation energy costs.

Strawbale insulation is 126 times less the embodied energy of fiberglass insulation and 487 times less than polystyrene.

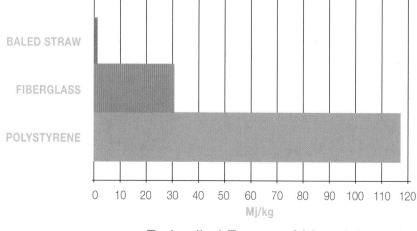

Embodied Energy of Materials

This energy embodied in manufactured materials is often a hidden cost to the environment. For instance, the high temperatures required to manufacture cement emit a significant portion of the world's global warming gases. Also, vast amounts of water are used to produce cement, and even more water is needed to turn cement to concrete.

Minimally processed natural materials have the least amount of embodied energy. Salvaged building materials of all kinds also score well in this category, as they replace the virgin materials and processing energy of new products, and reduce landfill costs. Local sourcing is best, as long distance transportation adds significantly to embodied energy.

## Energy Efficiency

The basic recipe for free solar comfort is to insulate the building envelope, include thermal mass inside, and place windows to face the winter sun. Climates, however, vary considerably. The key to successful design is to understand your building location, as well as the underlying qualities of your materials—and whether they work as mass or as insulation.

In the same way that achieving the most miles per gallon depends in part on how a hybrid car is driven, the performance of a hybrid house is enhanced by a smart homeowner—one who knows when to open or close insulating curtains and how to utilize the nighttime breeze in a summer cooling strategy.

Modern manufactured insulations such as fiberglass and foam are routinely used in conventional construction. While this may not change anytime soon, because of their high embodied energy and chemical composition, many health-conscious designers are seeking benign alternatives. This has created a market for a variety of natural, non-toxic insulations, including cellulose (recycled newspaper), mineral wool, cotton batt insulation, and straw bales.

Inside a well-insulated envelope, mass materials enhance comfort by keeping temperatures more constant. Mass works well in floors or walls, and even in ceilings between floors. There are a number of natural mass materials that are inexpensive and non-toxic, including stone, adobe, rammed earth, and cob. Even a thick coat of plaster on a strawbale wall adds up to a significant amount of mass. An added benefit over stud and drywall, is that mass walls significantly reduce sound transfer between rooms and floors.

Tile, brick, and concrete are also good thermal mass materials. While they have higher embodied energy, they also have the important quality of moisture resistance. They make good choices for foundations, floors, and countertops.

## Pleasing Aesthetics

Ideally, a hybrid house is a synergy of health, comfort, and beauty. The qualities of natural materials offer a type of aesthetic that resonates deep in human cellular memory. Handcrafted and full of texture, almost alive, a natural home invites the creative touch of the homeowner. And what could be more beautiful than something you made yourself?

When choosing building materials and systems for your hybrid house, combine quality ingredients with care and attention, enjoy the process, and savor the results.

sou

A hybrid home is a whole-systems design that relates and responds to its climate and location. As the name implies, a hybrid house is a thoughtful combination

# thwest

of construction materials and methods, selected for resource and energy efficiency. A hybrid design also harvests natural energy flows and is integrated with the landscape around it.

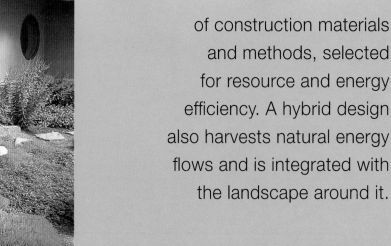

# off-the-grid
# strawbale
## home offers a vision of self-sufficiency

**Location:** Corrales, New Mexico

**Designer/Owner/Builder:** Ted Owens, design generalist

**Year Built:** 1998–2000

**Square Footage:** 830

**Bedrooms/Baths:** Loft bedroom, 1 bath

**Approximate cost:** $100/sq. ft. (including solar system, not including owner/builder labor)

**Climate:** High-altitude desert with hot summers and cold winters, seasonal heavy rains and occasional heavy snow potential

**Site Specifics:** Gently sloped lot with southern exposure

**Sustainable Strategies:** Passive solar design, strawbale exterior walls, corrugated metal roof, adobe interior mass walls, earth plasters, cellulose ceiling insulation, rubble trench foundation, radiant floor heat, salvaged oak flooring, double-pane low-E windows, photovoltaic solar panels, rainwater catchment and storage, gray-water system.

The compact cottage makes use of reused and natural materials, including adobes, salvaged oak flooring, surplus tile, and flagstone for window seats and shelves.

For owner and builder Ted Owens, his home is the culmination of years of work and several passions—for solar energy; for simple, elegant design; and for creative media-making. Even with the small size, the house turned into a massive project for a first-time owner/builder. The designer/filmmaker spent years researching and designing, two years building the house, and another year making an artful documentary of the step-by-step process.

Ted found inspiration in the traditional designs of northern New Mexico adobe homes, and in the book *A Pattern Language* by Christopher Alexander. "It makes you think about how the house flows and where your eye goes. Small spaces always have a view outside. Windows should

illuminate all rooms with natural light from two directions." Ted sought to design an aesthetic, ergonomic, and efficient home, and to demonstrate that livability is not dependent on size.

The resulting labor of love is a compact, finely crafted hybrid of timber, straw bales, adobe, and stone that is powered by the sun and collects and stores rainwater. Its solar orientation is enhanced by a thick adobe wall, concrete floors, and clay and gypsum plasters enclosed within 18-inch-thick strawbale walls (about R-30) and 15 inches of cellulose insulation in the ceiling (about R-40). This combination of south-facing windows, an insulated building envelope, and mass materials inside is the basic recipe for a comfortable and energy-efficient home.

## From the ground up, Ted made choices
# to minimize embodied energy

and maximize on-site resources. Utilizing a "rubble trench" foundation, he saved more than half of the concrete normally used to support a structure. He also plumbed the house to water the landscape with "gray water" from the shower and sink, which saves on both water and waste systems.

Ted chose "Energy Star" appliances for his kitchen, which lowered his need for electricity. He also became very conscious of contemporary electronics, which often suck electrical power even while they are turned off. This can spell disaster for an off-the-grid solar system.

To eliminate some of these "phantom loads," Ted installed his stereo and TV on a separate wall switch that he can manually turn off when not in use. A low-wattage lamp plugged into the same circuit serves as a reminder whether they are on or off.

Living off of the grid has helped Ted become more aware of resource conservation, and he found that small changes could have big results. This helped him develop new habits and a new ecological consciousness. This is one reason his video about the construction process of his home is called "Building with Awareness." The DVD shows step-by-step the path he took in reducing his home's carbon footprint almost to zero.

▲ ● ■ Rainwater harvested from the roof flushes the toilet and supplies cold water to the clothes washer and to a gardening spigot. Ted's 1,000-square-foot roof will capture 600 gallons of water from a 1-inch rain, which is stored in an underground cistern until needed.

# the "econest"
## a home that heals

**Location:** Tesuque, New Mexico

**Owners:** Amira and Darrell Ingram, proprietors of Casa Natura, a natural building supply store

**Architect:** Paula Baker-Laporte, FAIA

**Builder:** Robert Laporte

**Year Built:** 2005

**Square Footage:** 2,300 sq. ft. house and guest "casita"

**Bedrooms/Baths:** 3 bedrooms, 3 baths

**Approximate cost:** $250/sq. ft.

**Climate:** Dry high desert, hot summers, light snow in winter

**Site Specifics:** Almost flat lot with southern exposure

**Sustainable Strategies:** Timber frame, straw-clay walls with stone wainscoting, exterior plaster of brown local clay, interior plaster of white kaolin clay with mica and natural pigments, non-toxic finishes, metal roof with four-foot overhangs, skylights, radiant floor heat, masonry stove, stone and tile floors, slate countertops, south-facing passive solar orientation.

**LEFT:** Robert also built himself a large timber-framed workshop nearby, for a serene space to practice and teach his building craft.

**RIGHT:** An entry gate and covered walkway up to the front door make the approach to the home very private.

Architect Paula Baker-Laporte (primary author of *Prescriptions for a Healthy House*) and her husband, Robert Laporte (founder of the EcoNest Building Company), practice what they teach. Together they designed and built a serene compound of elegant Asian-influenced buildings north of Santa Fe, New Mexico, using healthful construction practices and natural materials.

Now, they live and work in solar-oriented timber-framed buildings of their own creation, which they call the "EcoNest."

Paula's interest in natural building began when her own health was compromised by multiple chemical sensitivities that developed from exposure to toxic materials on building sites. She met Robert at a natural house workshop

in Colorado in 1995, where he was advocating building with unprocessed traditional materials, including straw-clay walls and earthen plasters, which he believed has a beneficial effect on the health of the building's occupants.

Since then they have collaborated personally and professionally, developing the EcoNest concept by designing, building, and living in the houses they advocate. "Many features we first tried out on ourselves have now become standard in our clients' homes," says Paula. She believes that living in their "natural" houses actually helped her heal from her chemical sensitivities. In 2005, the couple co-authored *EcoNest: Creating Sustainable Sanctuaries of Clay, Straw and Timber.*

> I accept the challenge of sustainability, but I think we can do better and work toward ecological regeneration. Sustainability speaks of survival, but regeneration implies *thriving*.
>
> —Robert Laporte

Their Tesuque home, which was purchased by the Ingram family in 2006, includes a two-bedroom residence and a separate guest "casita" connected by a landscaped courtyard. The Ingrams, who moved from San Francisco to Santa Fe "to raise their two children in a wholesome environment," fill this comfortable and spacious home to the brim. Darrel makes his home office in the guest casita, and the children share one of the two bedrooms.

Darrel and his wife, Amira, a former publisher of "The Body-Mind Connection," own and operate Casa Natura ("the natural house") in Santa Fe. Their store stocks organic products for the home, including mattresses, cleaning products, and baby clothes. This health-conscious family appreciates the beautiful sunsets, the serene architecture and, especially, the healthful qualities of their EcoNest.

**FACING:** Tile, stone, slate, and other durable finishing materials require minimal maintenance.

**ABOVE:** A solar bump-out window wall is oriented due south, bringing warmth and light directly into the main living area. The thick stone windowsill and stone floors soak up the abundant winter sun, but overhangs provide shade for the walls in the summer.

**RIGHT:** The interior also has a Japanese feel. Shoji screens slide into pockets in the walls, lightly separating private and public spaces. The proportions are elegant yet modest.

s

If architects, builders, developers, and homeowners will make it a priority to improve energy efficiency in all new construction and remodeling projects

# outh

over the next two decades, the cumulative effect could turn our planet back from a climate in crisis, and onto a path toward true sustainability.

# soulful
## eco-renovation
# is faithful
## to historic
## neighborhood

**Location:** Takoma Park, Maryland

**Owner:** Bill Hutchins and Beth Knox

**Architect:** Bill Hutchins

**Builder:** Owners were general contractor

**Year Built:** 2005–2006

**Square Footage:** 700 sq. ft. existing home, with 1,400 sq. ft. two-story addition, plus a 650 sq. ft. basement rental apartment

**Climate:** Hot humid summers, occasional torrential rains

**Site Specifics:** Gently sloping urban lot

**Bedrooms/Baths:** 4 bedrooms, 2 1/2 baths

**Approximate cost:** $180 per sq. ft.

**Sustainable Strategies:** Reclaimed materials from deconstructed original home, other natural and salvaged materials, urban forestry, urban permaculture, natural cooling strategies, increased insulation, clay plasters, rainwater management, solar electric panels, hot water heating system, pellet stove, living roof.

**LEFT:** The backyard is an urban oasis.

**RIGHT:** The second-floor addition is visible from the street but blends right into the neighborhood, except for the rainbow of bright colors they chose to paint it, for its "happiness factor."

Years before he bought it, architect Bill Hutchins had strolled by the bright yellow bungalow many times on his way to visit a client. It was little more than "a shed with a kitchen tacked on the back," but its pleasant facade faced a shady street in the walkable  Takoma Park historic district. And it was conveniently located just minutes from downtown Washington, D.C., with a metro station just a block away. Somehow drawn to the house, Bill made a mental note and walked on.

House-hunting a few years later, he and his wife, Beth Knox, rediscovered this modest 700-square-foot cottage—a friend was buying it as an investment. "That's our house!" they told him, and a deal was struck. Bill and Beth spent the next two years designing, permitting, and

constructing an energy-efficient renovation that remained true to the neighborhood of century-old Victorian and bungalow homes.

Their home was originally built in 1910; it was one of the smallest homes on the street on a long, narrow lot. It included an upstairs bedroom with an illegal stairway and a small funky kitchen. Beth and Bill needed to construct enough room for three

teenagers and two home offices, so they knew they were in for a major project. Eventually they would add more than 2,000 square feet to the building.

An architect with a holistic approach, Bill formed his company, Helicon Works, in 1989 as a collaborative of professionals who could provide clients nearly any building service, from design and construction documents, to construction

management, to building cabinets, to landscaping and storm-water management. In 1998, while attending a nearby "natural building colloquium," he became excited by natural building "in a big way," and began including more natural materials and methods in his recommendations to clients.

So, naturally, when designing the renovation and expansion of his own home, Bill had many

▲ ● ■ **LEFT:** Bill usually meets with his clients and colleagues in the tall front room. The interior drywall walls are brightened with the Lazure technique of painting.

**BELOW:** A sitting room with strawbale walls offers a serene space for conversation or relaxation.

ideas he wanted to integrate, such as the straw-bale walls that enclose a cozy family room at the rear of the house. "This is the first permanent strawbale project so close to urban Washington," he said, "It's literally 500 feet to the border of the District of Columbia. I've been waiting for such an opportunity, and somehow it is my own home!"

Strict Takoma Park historic codes require that any changes visible from the street must be authentic to the existing architectural style. Bill and Beth proposed to retain the charming facade and front porch and expand the house 45 feet behind it into the large backyard. They stressed that their renovation would be ecological and energy-thrifty.

Bill's design responded to the regional climate—relatively humid with a mild heating

**BELOW:** Colorful hanging glass over the kitchen window maintains the pleasure of daylighting, while offering privacy.

**RIGHT:** Ceiling fans are installed throughout the home to create a cooling breeze. They use far less energy than air conditioning. Bill prefers to keep lights and fans separate, for versatility.

season and a long cooling season. "A house wants to act like a sundial, where different parts of the house get sun at different times of the day," explains Bill.

Of course, the house was already in place, oriented to the street, with the long wall facing southwest.

Sunshine coming from the west will rapidly heat a building in the afternoon, so Bill minimized southwest windows and put more windows on the southeast for solar gain, ventilation, and "enough windows for daylight." Other cooling strategies included tall ceilings, a central staircase to create a subtle "chimney effect," cross-ventilation in most rooms, ceiling and wall fans, and transom openings over doors to allow air to circulate between rooms.

They also got the okay to fill the southwest-facing roof with solar photovoltaic units, fitting enough collectors to generate 1.224 kilowatts of

electricity. "We're the only house that they allowed visible solar panels for," says Bill, but in fact the amorphous solar film, laminated to the standing seam metal roofing, is virtually invisible. The grid-tied system reduces the family electricity bill by about 25 percent.

To insulate the original frame walls, they added two inches of polyisocianurate foam (a bio-based spray foam) on the inside of the interior walls and the ceilings, which helped seal cracks and other minor air leaks that add up to compromise comfort and energy-efficiency. They then sheathed it on the inside with gypsum board (drywall).

In the new construction they filled the wall cavities and ceiling with blown-in cellulose. To match the original shiplap siding of the historic home, Bill found cedar planking that came from selective, horse-drawn logging, taken to an Amish mill.

the rice
hull house:
# a prototype
for coastal climates

**Location:** Washington, Louisiana

**Owner:** Rand Speyrer

**Designer:** Paul Olivier

**Builder:** Paul Olivier

**Year Built:** 2004

**Square Footage:** 2,300

**Climate:** Hot humid summers, mild winters; potential for violent storms, hurricanes, flooding

**Site Specifics:** Urban lot, elevated from the street

**Bedrooms/Baths:** 2 bedrooms, 3 baths

**Approximate cost:** $100/sq. ft.

**Sustainable Strategies:** Optimized wood-truss structural frame is filled with rice hulls for wall, floor, and ceiling insulation. Pier and beam foundation keeps structure above ground moisture and allows ventilation beneath the first floor. Wide porches and eaves shed rain, exterior shutters and storm door protect windows during violent storms, double doors increase insulation. Energy efficient cooling system.

One day in the spring of 2006, Rand Speyrer found himself in nearby historic Washington, where a charming Acadian-style home caught his eye. He thought, "That's the perfect house!"

Rand Speyrer used to live in New Orleans, but his apartment was destroyed in September 2005 by Hurricane Katrina. In advance of the storm, Rand evacuated to his parent's home in Opelousas, Louisiana, about 120 miles to the northwest. There he became a houseguest much longer than anyone would have imagined.

Fortunately, his employer allowed him to transfer to Opelousas, in St. Landry's Parish, where he grew up. Rand began driving around on weekends, looking for a house to buy. One day in the spring of 2006 he found himself in nearby historic Washington, where a charming Acadian-style home caught his eye. He thought, "That's the perfect house!" But, in the absence of a "for sale" sign, he drove away.

⚠ ● ■ **ABOVE:** The formal landscape and fountain create a
cooling effect on the property.

**RIGHT:** Unprocessed rice
hulls meet all of the safety
requirements for use as an
insulation, including fire and
mold resistance. Their insulation value is R-3 per inch.

As Rand tells the story,
"then I looked up my

# cousin Paul at
# his antique store,

and he invited me over to see the new house he had built. It turned out to be the same one I had just fallen in love with. I couldn't help but joke, 'You wouldn't think of selling this, would you?'" Synchronistically, Paul Olivier, designer, builder, and owner, had recently been contemplating a move from the area. The two cousins struck a deal, and Rand moved into his dream home a few months later.

Since he had no furniture, Rand acquired various antiques from his family to decorate the house. Then he went to work creating a lush landscape to complement his unconventional traditional home.

Unconventional, because inside this replica of a historic Acadian house, the walls, floors, and ceiling are insulated with 20 tons of compacted rice hulls. This insulation makes a huge difference in energy required to heat, and—in this hot, humid climate—to cool a building. As a result, Rand's typical monthly bill for electricity averages $50, compared to a neighbor's $600 electric bill.

Says Rand, "Once I have the house cooled down, it's comfortable for a couple of days, due to the excellent insulation of the rice hulls." Rand also is a smart homeowner. "I shut the air conditioning down each day when I go to work.

Also, I can choose to isolate one or two rooms and can just heat or cool the parts of the house that I am working in." He also practices passive cooling by opening the house up in the evening and turning on a fan to exchange with and capture the cool night air.

The vernacular design of the home, featuring an elevated first floor, wide porches, and storm shutters, makes perfect sense in this climate prone to severe storms and floods. Likewise, the durable corrugated metal roof and wood-composite siding shed precipitation, keeping the structure dry and snug. This innovative hybrid of old and new technologies is an eco-friendly model

for rebuilding along the devastated Gulf Coast.

Compared with so many who were displaced by Hurricane Katrina, Rand's story has a happy ending. Proud of his deep roots in French-speaking Cajun country, he has named his new home "Belle Vue." And he finds himself living comfortably-ever-after in the first-ever rice-hull house.

▲ ● ■ Having lost his possessions during Hurricane Katrina, Rand Speyrer filled his new home with family antiques and art.

idwest

Choices and decisions made while new buildings are designed and built will have long-lasting effects. An energy-efficient, healthy home, office, store, or factory not only benefits the initial owner but also future generations. Put in economic terms, what if we were to treat our life-support system—the earth—as an investment? What if we were to use the dividends and interest that nature provides without depleting the capital?

# the
# prairie
## hybrid house

**Location:** The Flint Hills of Southeast Kansas

**Owner:** Jane Koger

**Architect:** Stephen Lane, Lawrence, Kansas

**Builder:** Jerry Keller

**Interior Finishes:** Jann Jaggard

**Year Built:** 2000

**Square Footage:** 1,600

**Climate:** Hot humid summers, cold winters, windy year-round

**Site Specifics:** Rolling grassland, 32 inches of average annual rainfall

**Bedrooms/Baths:** 2 bedrooms/1 bath, plus loft bedroom

**Approximate Cost:** Not available

**Sustainable Strategies:** Salvaged lumber and limestone from an old barn used for structure, trim, stone walls, and floors. Native Indiangrass from the land was baled for the wall insulation. A 2 kW photovoltaic (PV) solar system and a 1 kW wind generator provide electricity. Fifteen solar thermal panels provide hot water; gray water from showers and sinks waters plants in the attached greenhouse; composting toilet.

Fourth-generation rancher Jane Koger's roots are deeply planted in the Flint Hills of Kansas. "I came back to Chase County to buy land and ranch," says Jane. "I was ranching on land that someone else held the lease on, and I wanted to have a little more 'control' over my future." After selecting a tract of rolling prairie land, she discovered during the title search that her great-grandparents, Emma and Ezra Beedle, had originally homesteaded the property in 1882. She had come home.

The beautiful, rolling Flint Hills contain some of the last remaining tallgrass prairie in North America. The vast prairies of the Midwest were first grazed by millions of buffalo before becoming a productive breadbasket for an emerging nation. This southeast corner of Kansas was mostly spared the plow, due to former oceans of limestone just below the sea of green grass. With mere inches of topsoil, the land was just too poor and rocky for farming.

When it came time to build her own house, Jane had already decided on strawbale walls to insulate her from the harsh, windy winters and the sweltering summers. To create the structure, her eyes fell on a neighbor's barn that was falling into disrepair. Put into service in 1910, its roof was now caving in and the owners didn't really need the barn anymore—what they wanted was a garage. Jane and friends deconstructed the large historic barn—a dusty, dirty, and heavy job—and salvaged the materials for her future home. Then she replaced the barn with the needed garage.

Their sweat and toil was rewarded with a large supply of used lumber—still with a lot of life left—and hand-cut limestone from the foundation. Long beams and planks of yellow pine were incorporated into the structure, floor, walls, and trim of Jane's new house, adding instant history and character.

Jane chose a building site with respect for the land and her impact on it. She located the house below the brow of a hill so as not to affect her neighbor's view. To keep a low profile and shelter the home from the cold north wind, its north wall is dug into the hillside. The home faces south for solar heating and offers an expansive view of the verdant grassland where her cattle graze.

She chose to generate her own energy for a similar reason. Says Jane, "I think I'm a regular person. The only reason I'm off the grid is that the REA [Rural Electrification Administration] was going to set electric poles all the way up to my house. I said, 'I don't think so . . . that would ruin my view!'"

Her home is powered by a hybrid system of 2 kilowatts of solar electric panels mounted on the garage, and a 1-kilowatt wind generator that together charge a large bank of batteries. Jane points out that she is following in the footsteps of settlers in the 1930s, who also used windmills before electricity came to rural Kansas. But her system can run all the normal appliances of modern life—a well pump, computers, TV, lights, and even a chest freezer. (Propane powers the refrigerator.)

In fact, sometimes more energy is generated than the batteries can store, so Jane diverts the excess to an electric hot water heater. This hot water—in addition to fifteen solar water panels on the roof—supplies domestic hot water, radiant floor heat, and the occasional whirlpool bath. Should the battery bank run low, she also has a gas-powered generator to keep the lights on until the next day, when sunshine or wind charges them up again.

▲ ● ■ Solar thermal panels on the roof heat water that is stored in a 350-gallon tank in the basement. Photovoltaic panels on the garage and a wind generator provide electric power for this off-the-grid modern homestead.

In their life on the prairie,
Jane and her partner,

# Marva Weigelt,
## face the same

formidable weather as her ancestors did. The
worst weather for them is freezing rain—it
gradually attaches to the blades and freezes up
the wind generator. Some winters they will stack
big hay bales along the outside of the north wall
to insulate further against the frigid wind. They
find their radiant floor heat keeps them more
comfortable than forced-air heat. In the summer
they sometimes use a small air conditioner
during the hottest weather.

Jane attributes their frugal comfort to the
insulation power of the straw bales. "One of the
coldest winters ever, I called my architect and
said, 'Steve, did I ever tell you how great this
house is?'"

Though there is plenty of straw in the region,
Jane baled dried Indiangrass from her own
land. "We made the tightest bales we could and,
because I knew how to adjust the machine, I
went ahead and made half-bales and quarter-
bales to save time later in stacking. I called my
sister and said, 'I just baled my house today.'"

Jane hired local contractors and artisans to
help her build a strong, simple house based on a
friend's clerestory design, which brings light and
warmth into the north rooms. The exposed post-
and-beam framework is filled in with bales, and
the roof is insulated with salvaged 4 x 8 sheets of
Styrofoam and conventional fiberglass insulation.
Interior partition walls separate the space into

▲●■ Barn-wood trim,
native stone,
antiques, and found
objects ensure a
rustic and highly
personal décor.

In Case of Fire Break Glass!

rooms without ceilings—above the rooms the open space allows air circulation for cooling. This allows sounds to freely travel through the space as well.

Salvaged lumber ensures a rustic interior, which is accented by colorful gypsum interior plaster. Often, the finish work required creative solutions, like grouting the wood-plank floor with sawdust and oil sealer. Barn-wood trim, native stone, antiques, and found objects personalize the decor throughout. Still, Jane apologizes for its homespun character, "Ranch life is chunky . . . we just live here. We'd both rather be outside."

Deeply conservation minded, Jane and Marva are helping to restore nesting habitat for the endangered prairie chicken in partnership with the U.S. Fish and Wildlife Service and the Nature Conservancy. This includes discouraging tree growth in the grasslands. And every spring they burn a

**LEFT:** South-facing clerestory windows bring light and winter heat deep into the north rooms. The final "color coat" of cement-lime stucco is still to be applied. The rough coat shows the result of many hands helping at Jane's plastering parties.

**ABOVE:** Except for the bathroom, rooms are partitioned off without ceilings, allowing air flow for cooling ventilation. Sounds also flow through this open space.

**LEFT:** The bathroom features custom tile work, native limestone from the barn foundation, and a whirlpool tub that makes use of solar-heated hot water.

**BELOW LEFT:** The guest bedroom mimics the intense colors of a prairie sunrise.

**BELOW:** The composting toilet storage chamber is cranked every five days and is emptied every ten days.

**RIGHT:** The wheelchair-accessible living room features antiques and old barn wood for character. The wood stove is used for backup heat, fueled by hackberry and oak harvested from the fence rows.

portion of their pastures to simulate the effects that natural fires once had on this sea of grass.

"We are presently working on an experiment in three of our pastures," says Jane. "Each pasture is about 900 acres in size, and we burn 300 acres of each pasture, each year. In a three-year period, the entire pasture is burned. And we graze each pasture differently—one has yearling cattle on it for 90 days, one has yearling cattle for 180 days, and one has cows year-round."

Jane's herd is relatively small, numbering about a hundred head. This is plenty to manage, as they are busy all spring being midwife to the heifers, ready and able to turn a crossways calf around in the birth canal. The cows will usually calve year after year, contentedly munching on the Indiangrass, bluestem, and switchgrass of this lush landscape. Jane and Marva call their

cows by name—Winnie, Twanda, Merrilee—but not the young steers and heifers they are fattening for sale. The nameless yearlings are sold in the winter, except for a couple to provide grass-fed beef for their freezer and a few friends' tables.

A life on the land requires a constant awareness of the weather—especially if your electricity depends on the sun shining and the wind blowing. Fortunately, their off-the-grid energy systems work, and the sturdy strawbale and timber-frame walls stand up ably against the Midwest winter extremes.

And Jane is happy to report, "It's been a wonderful summer weather-wise—not too hot and plenty of moisture. We've found some small areas of big bluestem that are taller than the [Kawasaki] Mule! That's certainly a sign of a good year on the prairie."

# canadian couple
# creates
## a healthful haven

**Location:** Bancroft, Ontario, Canada

**Owner/Builders:** Patrick Marcotte and Sherri Smith

**Architect:** Linda Chapman

**Ground Source Heating System:** Next Energy

**Year Built:** 1999

**Square Footage:** 2,800

**Bedrooms/Baths:** 3 bedrooms, 2 baths, plus music studio, workshop and 2-car garage

**Approximate cost:** $75 per square foot, not counting owners' labor

**Climate:** Cold, wet, heavy snowfall

**Site Specifics:** wooded lot near a river

**Sustainable Strategies:** Post-and-beam frame with strawbale infill walls, frost-protected shallow foundation, ground-source heat pump that heats in-floor hydronic (radiant) heat, lime and gypsum plasters, mineral paints, low-E windows, strawboard cabinets with bamboo laminate, living roof on garden shed.

**LEFT:** A charming garden shed is topped with a living roof.

**RIGHT:** The skilled owner-builders created their country home from local, natural materials.

**BELOW RIGHT:** Strawbale walls provide super insulation as well as soundproofing for the music studio on one end of this comfortable family home.

Dissatisfied with being suburban commuters in an increasingly toxic environment, Sherri Smith and her husband, Patrick Marcotte, decided to lead a more sane and sustainable lifestyle. They purchased a piece of wooded property along a lake in rural Ontario and worked with architect Linda Chapman to design a healthy, eco-friendly home for their family. "One visit to a strawbale home she designed, and we were hooked!" says Patrick.

To save on the cost of construction, they decided to build it themselves. Patrick had remodeled homes in college and so had developed considerable building skills. Together, he and Sherri researched and made choices that would result in an affordable, energy-efficient, and healthful living

space. Then they spent months on their property, overseeing subcontractors and getting hands-on experience, building their home from the ground up.

The cold winters of Canada require a well-insulated building envelope, which they achieved with a frost-protected shallow foundation, strawbale walls, and cellulose ceiling insulation. A ground source heat pump provides an efficient heat supply,

linked with an in-floor radiant heating system.

After their creative learning experience on their own house, the couple started their own company, HavenCraft Natural Homes. Says Patrick, "In building this home, we have drastically reduced the amount of energy we use and have the great joy of being able to live in close contact with nature and its cycles. Also, I rediscovered that I really love building and couldn't remember why I'd ever left it."

The Canadian couple now uses their expertise with healthy building products and energy-efficient systems by consulting, managing, building, teaching, and leading work "bees" for clients.

▲●■ **FACING:** Plastered walls can be a canvas for artistic expression.

**LEFT:** Sherri Smith and Patrick Marcotte work together designing and building healthy, energy-efficient homes in Ontario, Canada.

**ABOVE:** Patrick builds and repairs stringed instruments, and plays music in a home studio.

**ABOVE:** A custom dresser was handcrafted by Patrick from bamboo and non-toxic strawboard.

**RIGHT:** Inside their comfortable home, Sherri and Patrick "have the great joy of being able to live in close contact with nature and its cycles."

**FACING:** Sculpted bale walls can offer an organic aesthetic.

We have
drastically reduced the amount of
energy we use and have the great joy of
being able to live in close contact
with nature and its cycles.

nor

While conservation in all aspects of industrialized society will have an impact, buildings account for roughly half of all energy consumed in first

# theast

world countries, compared to 26 percent used by transportation. By far the largest amount of energy use is in the operation of our buildings, primarily for heating and cooling.

Photograph by Sarah Machtey

a tale of two
# families
in new york ecovillage

**Location:** Ithaca, New York

**Duplex Owners:** Joe and Michelle Nolan, and Graham O, with her partner, Otto

**Architect:** Michael McDonough

**Builders:** Sarah Highland and Aaron Dennis, contractors; Paul Lacinski, strawbale and plaster sub-contractor; masonry stove installed by Norbert Senf

**Year Built:** Completed in 2003

**Square Footage:** Duplex includes 1,200 sq. ft. living space for the Nolans, plus their 600 sq. ft. basement rental unit. Graham O's home is 1,100 sq. ft., plus a 400 sq. ft. basement laundry room.

**Bedrooms/Baths:** Each unit 3 bedrooms, 2 baths

**Approximate cost:** $200 per sq. ft., 2.5 kW grid-tied solar electric system per home, shared solar hot water system

**Climate:** Hot, humid summers; freezing winters with heavy snowfall

**Site Specifics:** Sloping site. Neighboring homes are close on both sides.

**Sustainable Strategies:** Space saving duplex with exterior and common walls of straw bales stacked vertically within a lumber "balloon" frame, lime-stabilized clay plaster with vermiculite, natural pigments and stains, masonry wood stove supplemented with radiant floor heat and radiators, triple-pane low-E windows, durisol foundation, cellulose ceiling insulation, 2.5 kW photovoltaic solar electric system, solar hot water collectors, reclaimed barn-wood floor and timber frame, salvaged sinks, doors, and cabinets, local slate floor, employed local artisans.

On a cross-country vacation,
Joe and Michelle Nolan
# discovered an

emerging "ecovillage" on the outskirts of Ithaca, New York, and bought a membership on the spot. The Silicon Valley, California, couple had imagined raising children in a sustainable community, and the EcoVillage at Ithaca matched their long-term vision. They teamed up with a prospective neighbor, Graham O, to create adjoining residences.

To create a successful duplex, the design process must consider the needs and dreams of two owners and an architect. Seeing eye-to-eye was sometimes tricky. The owners were eager to try eco-friendly straw bales as insulation walls, with a cozy interior aesthetic, while the architect had a more contemporary vision. Still, working to achieve consensus is one of the goals of community living, and the collaboration remained friendly.

Since New York has abundant timber resources, they all easily agreed on the structural system, a hybrid of a traditional timber frame, exposed where appropriate for aesthetics, and a wood-thrifty "balloon frame" system hidden inside the walls. Insulating straw bales were installed vertically between the supporting wall trusses, creating a solid two-story duplex, with a basement on the south side.

So, a California family became the first to create a strawbale house in the city limits of Ithaca, New York. The event was clearly special. Seventy people showed up to help raise the timber frame—in January!

**RIGHT:** The EcoVillage at Ithaca currently includes sixty homes, an organic farm, playgrounds, a swimming pond, and other natural areas on a 175-acre site. The award-winning buildings at EVI use eco-friendly strategies to achieve energy efficiency and overall sustainability.

**BELOW RIGHT:** The tall strawbale walls are protected on the south, east, and west with a wood siding of hemlock. Note the solar hot water panels on the roof.

A compostable house feels
good to us. For me, the straw bales, timber
frame, and masonry stove were
the elements that made it worthwhile.

—Joe Nolan

The water in the hot water heating system is shared by both sides of the duplex. The Nolans are delighted with their choice of efficient radiant heat. Joe remembers the forced air furnace in their former home as unpleasant. "It was noisy, always coming on and off, and it had cold spots, so it was hard to keep comfortable." The "hydronic" radiant-floor system is heated by a high-efficiency condensing natural gas boiler,

and the hot water is circulated through "Pex" pipe, a durable and strong polyethylene tubing.

For domestic hot water, evacuated-tube collectors preheat a 120-gallon water storage tank, often to 100-plus degrees Fahrenheit. Joe estimates that these solar thermal collectors provide about 70 percent of their showers, laundry, dishwashing, etc., and sometimes preheat the radiant floor loop. The more expensive

evacuated tube collectors can create hot water
even on cloudy days—a distinct advantage in the
New England climate.

The 2.5 kW photovoltaic system for each side
of the duplex creates enough electrical energy
for the Nolans' busy lifestyle, and then some.
The excess power their system creates goes
back into "the grid" and helps power their neighbors' homes.

**FACING:** Local artisans
were employed for many
finishing details, giving
the homes a hand-
crafted look and feel.
(Photograph by Sarah
Machtey)

**ABOVE:** Inviting and
useful front porches
protect the north-facing
front doors and lime-
plastered strawbale
walls of the duplex.

**RIGHT:** In Graham O's half of the duplex, this earthen sculpture is the artistic centerpiece and metaphorical heart of the home. (Artist, Sarah Machtey.)

**FACING, ABOVE:** Natural, non-toxic materials used in construction help to ensure healthful indoor air quality. (Photograph by Sarah Machtey)

**FACING, BELOW:** Soakers in this pedestal bathtub enjoy a view through triple-pane low-E windows. They open to provide ventilation when desired.

## The Nolans also commissioned a
# handsome masonry stove

that supplies up to 90 percent of their heat from wood, which in their region is a renewable resource. In the winter the family typically needs to burn four to five logs a day to keep the temperature up. The thermal mass of the stove, the flagstone floor, and the thick plaster covering the bale walls absorb and store the heat from the fireplace.

For summer cooling, the family makes use of nighttime ventilation, which means opening windows both on the first floor (cool air intake) and the second floor (to naturally vent the warm air). Windows are closed in the morning, before it heats up outdoors.

The Nolan's "wabi sabi" aesthetic embraces the rustic elegance of natural and reclaimed materials. Employing local artisans to craft functional elements like twig railings and stained glass added beauty at a reasonable cost. "It was fun to incorporate the salvaged things we collected over time," says Michelle.

While it was gratifying to stack bales and plaster by hand, the Nolans appreciated how a mechanical mortar mixer and stucco sprayer helped speed up the building process. Graham O's "plaster experiment wall" in the basement was invaluable in deciding textures and colors, and developing a recipe for durability with local clays.

wes

# t coast

Reducing consumption is the quickest way to begin reversing the trend and start becoming a "carbon neutral" society. Both society and consumers benefit from conservation

by saving the cost of energy not consumed. Doesn't that mean we have to give up things? Not necessarily. We can begin by reducing the amount of things we waste.

# sustainable living
## in the city

**Location:** Capitola, California

**Owners:** Kristin and Mark Sullivan

**Architect:** Kelly Lerner, One World Design

**Builder:** Michele Landegger and Debrae Lopes, Boa Constructor Building and Design

**Year Built:** 2001–2002

**Square Footage:** 1,520

**Climate:** California coastal, frequent morning clouds and clear afternoons

**Site Specifics:** Narrow, flat urban lot

**Bedrooms/Baths:** 2 bedrooms, 2 baths

**Approximate cost:** $200/sq. ft.

**Sustainable Strategies:** Passive solar design, grid-intertied solar electric system, solar hot water panels for domestic hot water and radiant heat, on-demand backup water heater, stained concrete floors, interior clay plasters, strawbale wall and cellulose ceiling insulation, salvaged lumber, doors and fixtures, certified sustainably harvested lumber, energy-efficient appliances, compact fluorescent bulbs, a rainwater catchment system, drought-tolerant native landscaping, permeable driveway.

# Instead of building their dream home on pristine
# country acreage, eco-conscious

**RIGHT:** The south exposure is faced with windows, allowing the sun to stream in during the heating season, where its heat is absorbed into the thermal mass of the floors and plasters.

**BELOW RIGHT:** The higher up-front cost of the solar systems keeps the Sullivans' monthly energy bills incredibly low—they pay an average of about $10 per month for all utilities combined.

teachers Kristin and Mark Sullivan chose to build in the city so they could live close to urban amenities and culture. But they decided to "walk their talk" by building a super-energy-efficient house with solar heating and electricity. The result is a model of sustainability that allows them to enjoy a comfortable California lifestyle with a miniscule energy bill.

Just blocks from a sandy beach, they deconstructed a run-down cottage on a narrow lot to build an inviting Craftsman-style home. Passive energy efficiency is concealed within the attractive design. Siting the house at the minimum five-foot setback along the north side of the narrow 45 x 100 foot lot allows more living space on the south for maximum daylight and solar heat in the winter.

Photovoltaic and solar thermal collectors on

The contemporary kitchen features Energy Star appliances.

the roof provide nearly all of the power and hot water they need. These systems, in concert with passive solar design and super-insulated walls and ceilings, translate to rock-bottom energy bills: their monthly electric and gas use combined averages about ten dollars per month.

The Sullivans also practice thrifty habits that add up to save energy. They turn off lights when they leave the room, and their computer and peripherals are all on power strips, which allows them to eliminate the "phantom loads" created by internal power draws and indicator

lights that seem to be on all modern appliances, office equipment, and electronic gadgets.

During their design phase, they discovered the cozy feeling of strawbale walls, but they were warned that bales were too bulky for urban building. Also, they had the same concerns as many other people—fire, bugs, mold, and earthquakes (Capitola is a seismic zone 4). Despite their fears, and reassured by their architect and builders, they decided the insulation value and soundproofing of bale walls would be an asset.

The Sullivans' passion for green building kept them pushing the boundaries of the conventional subcontractors involved with their home. They encouraged the concrete company to increase the amount of fly ash (a replacement for cement) in their slab, up to 40 percent without problems. And during

construction, Mark and Kristin invited friends and family to join in on strawbale and earth-plastering parties, which developed a wonderful camaraderie.

Now, the Sullivans continue to educate, opening their home for a guided tour every month to neighbors, students, and others

who hear about it by word of mouth. Typically twenty to seventy people take the tour. "We get people who come and say, 'I put that bale there. I plastered that wall.' People have a stake in your home," Mark explains. "We're planting seeds."

**LEFT:** The thickness of bale walls allow for wide sills and window seats.

**ABOVE:** Luscious micaceous clay plaster adorns the interior strawbale walls. Ferrous sulfate, a benign and inexpensive agricultural fertilizer, was used to stain the exterior lime/cement stucco and cement floors.

# creativity
# transforms
## an "unbuildable" lot

**Location:** Laguna Beach, California

**Owners:** Chris and Becky Prelitz

**Designer/Builder:** Chris Prelitz

**Year Built:** 2000–2003

**Square Footage:** 2,100 sq. ft. two-story, with 1000 sq. ft. garage/studio in daylit basement

**Bedrooms/Baths:** 3 bedrooms used as 1 bedroom 2 offices/3 bath

**Approximate cost:** $400,000

**Climate:** Temperate coastal southern California

**Site Specifics:** On a hillside above the Pacific Coast, a ravine filled in by an adjoining landslide created a barren funnel with a storm drain at the lowest point, considered an "unbuildable" lot.

**Sustainable Strategies:** Southern orientation for passive heating, passive cooling with overhangs and operable skylights, natural light from two directions in all rooms, "para-lams"—structural beams made of scrap wood, strawbale west wall, salvaged lumber, doors and sink, fireplace and in-floor radiant heating downstairs/passive heat upstairs, passive thermosyphon hot water loop, photovoltaic electric system with energy-saving lighting throughout, durable corrugated metal roofing, exterior lime wash, low-VOC interior paints, rainwater and gray-water use in landscape.

**PREVIOUS PAGE:** Creative homeowners transformed this Laguna Beach hillside from a "barren brown funnel" to a lush landscape that soaks up rainwater and produces food.

**RIGHT:** The moist landscape combined with fire-resistant building materials, such as the tile roof, slate siding, and stuccoed exterior, minimize danger from wildfires.

**BELOW RIGHT:** Coastal Southern California enjoys a climate that celebrates indoor/ outdoor living.

A building contractor by trade, Chris was able
# to buy his own lot in pricey

Laguna Beach at a bargain because it looked like "a barren brown funnel." His strategy was to plant the garden first so that when the house was finished, it would have a view of lush foliage. Oriented to the south for solar gain and to catch the prevailing breezes, the well-insulated design was able to pass California's strict Title 24 energy code without any heat source upstairs, other than the sun.

Initially, Chris terraced the steepest part of the site with retaining walls built from "urbanite" (free concrete chunks retrieved from demolition sites). Then, on a crescent-shaped sliver of high ground, he began building a three-story wooden structure, including a daylit basement. Chris designed the house

without load-bearing interior walls so it could be flexible and grow "organically" as he and his wife Becky live in the space.

This flexibility also allowed him to save money by incorporating reclaimed materials and treasures salvaged from remodeling jobs, including lumber, vintage doors, slate shingles, antique sinks, redwood decking, and more scavenged "urbanite" for patio paving. Even the landscape of drought-tolerant native vegetation is mulched with chipped waste wood from local tree trimmers.

The interior is enhanced by natural light and the artistic use of natural materials, many of which were salvaged from other homes being deconstructed.

Cooling ocean breezes in winter can be warded off by an occasional fire in the fireplace.

Taking advantage of the generally pleasant coastal

# California climate, the hillside

home allows casual indoor/outdoor living. However, the afternoon summer sun can often cause a house to overheat. For this reason, Chris reduced windows to the west and chose to insulate the west wall with thick straw bales. With the help of low-energy-use ceiling fans, the hillside home ventilates efficiently through the night, creating comfortable interior temperatures all summer, without air conditioning.

After nearly two decades working as a "green" contractor, Chris has become a sustainability consultant. He now advises commercial and residential clients about cost-effective strategies to reduce their energy use and create a healthy home.

eu

There is a great peace of mind in knowing that a hybrid house is a healthy house. In the same way that junk food is bad to ingest, junk construction is harmful to live inside.

**rope**

Replacing known toxic building materials with less-processed natural materials is better for the planet, and for people, too. After all, how much is your health worth?

pre-fabricated
design and
# comfort
converge in
austrian passivhaus

**Location:** Wienerherberg, Austria

**Owner:** Angelika Rutard

**Architect:** Winfried Schmelz

**Builder:** Proksch Weilguni

**Year Built:** 2004

**Square Footage:** 182 sq. m. (1,958 sq. ft.) with a 45 sq. m. (484 sq. ft.) deck

**Climate:** Hot, humid summers; cold, partly sunny, partly cloudy in winter

**Site Specifics:** Flat building site in suburban neighborhood

**Cost:** 210,000 Euro (about $294,000)

**Sustainable Solutions:** Prefabricated wall panels insulated with straw bales assembled on site, passive solar design, minimal use of concrete in the foundation, airtight construction, rain-screen wall protection.

▲●■ **ABOVE:** A mezzanine floor features the "relaxing room" overlooking the backyard and pool. It could also function as a home office.

**ABOVE RIGHT:** All windows have interior roll-down shades and exterior shutters, remote controlled from the inside. The thoughtful design includes both fixed windows for view, light, and heat gain, and some that open to catch prevailing breezes.

Angelika Rutard bought a large lot in a development east of Vienna in 2003 and began working with her architect, Winfried Schmelz, that December. Construction on the house started in March. Because of the high water table of the site, complications with supporting columns caused a delay of two months. Still, Angelika moved into her new home in June 2004, after just six months from design to completion. This

fast-track building schedule was made possible in part by a simple design, thorough drawings, and insulated structural panels prefabricated in a workshop, transported to and efficiently assembled on site.

A contemporary cube design, the modest two-bedroom, two-bath home makes efficient use of an 8 x 12-meter footprint—approximately 2,000 square feet (outside dimensions), plus a

45-square-meter (152 square-foot) deck. The exterior is finished with a screen of wooden slats, both decorative and practical—the self-draining "rain screen" intercepts precipitation, breaking the force of stormy weather before it makes contact with the house. It is also made from larch, a local, rot-resistant wood that should last for many decades.

# The foundation
## beneath the structure
# consists of four
# concrete beams

1 foot wide, 2 feet high, and 26 feet long. Prefabricated panels that form the walls, floor, and ceiling were built at a factory, brought to the site on a large truck, and erected in three days with the help of a construction crane. The 45-centimeter or 18-inch-thick panels were built with a core of insulating straw bales sandwiched between oriented strand board (OSB) made from local birch and larch trees. The insulation value of these panels is u - 0,13 W/mK, which translates to an R-value of 43.7!

Where the walls, floor, ceiling, doors, and windows come together, there is potential for air leakage. These joints were carefully sealed, creating a tight building envelope that reduces energy loss. To maximize free solar energy, the south wall is filled with high-efficiency windows, while on the cold north there are no windows. To control potential overheating, both east and

▲●■ **RIGHT:** Tilt-and-turn doors and windows allow superb flexibility for homeowners to adjust access and airflow.

west faces incorporate only two small windows each. This efficient design meets strict German "Passivhaus" standards, which require energy savings of 75 percent or more over conventional European buildings.

The super-insulated airtight envelope and solar design allowed the architect to eliminate a conventional heating system. Angelika lives comfortably with a small wood-burning stove. During a cold winter, the minimum indoor temperature she experienced was 20 degrees Celsius (68 degrees Fahrenheit), despite extreme temperatures outside.

In the case of too much sun, Angelika can control the amount of light that floods inside and prevent overheating with interior blinds and motorized exterior shades. In the summer, a 5-foot (1.5-meter) roof overhang shades the south-facing glass. She can also enhance her ventilation comfort by opening windows and doors. In the winter the fresh air exchange automatically passes through a heat-recovery ventilation system.

LEFT: A wood stove in the living room supplies the occasional additional heat required; otherwise, the sun does it all.

RIGHT: An interior window wall allows plenty of light into the bedroom and gives it a greater feeling of space.

The expansive view to the south includes Angelika's verdant backyard and the sky, but just a sliver of the street. These large windows, and the clever use of an inside "window wall," enhances the sense of space in this compact home and fills the interior with natural light.

Architect Schmelz also designed the interior spaces. He chose natural finishes, primarily for healthy indoor air quality. The inside sheathing of the straw panels (underneath the wooden wall finishes) is a moisture-tolerant, fire-resistant, non-toxic chipboard called heraclite, which is finished with lime plaster. The few interior partition walls are wood-framed, with local larch wood and trim, and finished with white casein paint.

Angelika is thrilled with the style, comfort, livability, and energy efficiency of her contemporary, cutting-edge Passivhaus. When asked what, if anything, she would change, Angelika mused, "Perhaps it could be a bit bigger."

# a natural
# remodel
## in northern italy

**Location:** Merano, Bolzano Province, Italy

**Owners:** Walter Mair and Johanna Mair-Hofer

**Architect:** Margareta Schwarz, PhD

**Builder:** Anton Schotzer

**Year Built:** 2006

**Square Footage:** 142 sq. m. living area (1,528 sq. ft.) plus 31 sq. m. gallery (334 sq. ft.) plus 39 sq. m. roofed balcony (420 sq. ft.)

**Climate:** Alpine/Mediterranean, 300 meters (1000 feet) above sea level

**Site Specifics:** Attic apartment of existing brick, with a concrete roof

**Bedrooms/Baths:** 1 bedroom, 2 baths

**Approximate cost:** 1,500 Euro/sq. m. (about 150 Euro/sq. ft. or $210/sq. ft. U.S. equivalent)

**Sustainable Strategies:** Solar design enhanced with interior walls of high-mass unfired clay bricks; natural, non-toxic building materials—wood, straw, clay, glass; daylighting with windows and skylights; rainwater harvesting; radiant heat, powered by solar thermal panels; insulating the top floor saves energy throughout the existing home.

# After raising two daughters in a sturdy brick house,

empty-nesters Johanna and Dr. Walter Mair (a dentist) decided they wanted to build a different home for this new stage in their lives. Yet they were very fond of their land and location in a beautiful fruit-growing valley below the Italian Alps. After consulting with their architect, Dr. Margareta Schwarz, they decided to replace the roof on their existing home and renovate the cold, dark attic into contemporary living quarters for themselves.

In contrast to the existing garret space, Walter and Johanna wanted to enjoy warm, cozy, light-filled rooms and the spectacular view to the south. Architect Schwarz suggested a wall of south-facing glass opening onto a balcony sheltered by the protective overhangs of a vaulted

roof with skylights. She also proposed building with natural materials throughout in order to maintain a healthy indoor environment.

Margareta also introduced the idea of using straw bales to insulate the new walls and roof. Despite their unfamiliarity with strawbale construction, the Mairs had great confidence in their architect and agreed with this and most of her choices. The client/architect collaboration proved to be fun and fruitful throughout the design and six-month construction process.

After the demolition of the existing roof and attic apartment, carpenters built a wooden framework for the new apartment from structural beams of laminated spruce, with formaldehyde-free glue. They filled the framework with standard straw bales (35 x 45 x 100 centimeters or 14 x 18 x 39 inches) placed "on edge." Above the walls they constructed a very unusual "monastery style" vaulted roof, which proved challenging for the carpenters, who found it difficult to build the complex curved structure.

Above this vaulted ceiling, more straw bales were placed for insulation, followed by wood decking, then a vapor permeable radiant barrier, and finally a tile roof. Safely under cover, the interior walls were built with extruded clay blocks set in clay mortar. Next, all the utilities were installed, including a solar water-heating system. Then the windows, doors, and floors were completed, and the strawbale and clay walls received three coats of clay plaster.

Before the renovation, the third floor was little more than an attic. (Photo courtesy of Margareta Schwarz.)

▲●■ **ABOVE:** The third-floor addition has reduced the home's former energy consumption by 75 percent. This satisfies the strict "climate protocol" of the Province of Bolzano for new construction.

**RIGHT:** Using straw bales to insulate the third-floor walls and ceilings provides a U-value calculated at 0.13W/m²K (equivalent to R-43.7). (Photo courtesy of Margareta Schwarz.)

## The wall colors were created by mixing natural colored clays

red, yellow, brown, and tan—with finely chopped straw and mica (vermiculite) for texture and sparkle. Small chips of lapis lazuli and turquoise set into the clay add colored accents.

On the outside, bale walls were covered with diagonal strips of wood, with gaps for "breathability," then plates of heraclite (a fire-resistant wall sheathing) before being finished with a vapor-permeable lime plaster.

A unique circular staircase leads to a gallery level that is a spectacular luxury: a skylit library replete with stylish, comfortable reading chair and a glass floor. Overhead the vaulted wooden ceiling shelters the space below while offering glimpses of the sky above. In fact, every space allows the homeowners some view of the picturesque valley surrounding them.

Despite the Alps looming nearby, the winters in Merano are not extremely cold. The region is,

in fact, sheltered from the northern wind by the Alps and tempered by warm air from southern Italy. Nighttime low temperatures in winter normally hover around freezing.

Nonetheless, the Mairs' remodelled home is noticeably more comfortable with significantly less energy use—down 75 percent from former consumption! Energy-saving effects are influenced by solar gain, airtight construction, the tempering mass of the interior clay brick walls, and, of course, the strawbale insulated roof and walls. Like a wool hat, they create a snug cap atop the three-story home.

▲●■ The meandering clayblock
walls are finished with
a textured earthen
plaster—even in the
kitchen and bathrooms.

 **FACING:** The overall effect of the organically shaped rooms, natural light and materials, and contemporary design is relaxing and soothing.

# A spectacular luxury: a skylight library replete with stylish, comfortable reading chair and a glass floor.

Starting from scratch on the third floor allowed Margareta to design sound attenuation between floors. Beneath the new walnut-plank flooring, soft plasterboard and marble sand absorb normal living sounds, aided by a noise reduction foil on the concrete ceiling below.

After the remodel was complete, the Mairs' daughter moved back into the family home with her husband and daughter, comfortably occupying the second floor. Johanna and Walter feel like royalty living above in their new contemporary apartment. Friends at first questioned why the Mairs chose to climb to the top floor to live, until they entered the luxurious light-filled space and beheld the view.

# jumbo bales
# stack up
## in the swiss alps

**Location:** Disentis, Switzerland

**Owner:** Urs and Christiane Braun-Dubuis

**Architect/Builder:** Werner Schmidt, Trun, Switzerland

**Year Built:** 2002

**Square Footage:** 110 sq. m. (about 1,200 sq. ft.)

**Bedrooms/Baths:** 2 bedrooms, 2 baths

**Approximate cost:** 500,000 Swiss Francs (about $460,000)

**Climate:** Cold, sunny winters, heavy snowfall

**Site Specifics:** Steep rocky slope, 1,300 m. (4,265 ft.) above sea level

**Sustainable Strategies:** Load-bearing walls of jumbo straw bales, conventional strawbale insulation under the wooden floor, and two layers of conventional strawbale insulation above the ceiling. Most woodwork inside and out utilizes a local spruce (tichte). The pier foundation of concrete-filled tubes minimizes site impact on the steep slope. Passive solar design meets more than 90 percent of heating needs. Motorized exterior window shades control overheating.

# grandeur and
# treachery

The Swiss Alps
epitomize the

▲●■ The home's stripped-
down elegance reflects
its simplicity: walls of
glass on the south and
super-insulation in the
floors, walls, and ceilings.

of alpine living. Snow-packed glaciers tower over the greenest grass-covered slopes in the summer, while winters may top everything with meters of snow. The alpine home of Urs Braun and Christiane Dubuis was built to withstand these elements and is amazingly comfortable without a conventional heating system. How can this be?

The deep snow of the Alps creates the headwaters that feed the mighty Rhine River. Yet it is seldom foggy or completely cloudy, and the sun shines most winter days. Architect Werner Schmidt's design premise was that this abundant winter sun, combined with a super-insulated building envelope, could provide adequate heat for comfortable living.

"In Disentis it is often minus 20 degrees to minus 30 degrees Celsius (-4 to -22 degrees Fahrenheit), but if the sun shines, it's no problem," says Werner. And he has confirmed his theory with the insulating power of load-bearing straw bales. But not just any bales—jumbo bales.

The size of these bales is startling. They average 250 x 125 x 70 cm (8 x 4 x 3 feet). They have a huge insulating power too. The 4-foot-wide bale has a European "U-value" of approximately 0.05 w/m2K, which in the U.S. converts to a whopping R-value of 113.4! Werner calculated that this power of insulation could collect and hold enough heat from the sun to keep his clients warm without supplemental heat.

But Urs and Christiane were not completely convinced of their architect's calculations and requested a wood stove be installed. And they stacked up several cords of wood for the first winter, just in case. To their surprise, the passive solar design and super-insulated building envelope functions so well, a wood fire is almost never needed. Over six winters they have burned only half of the wood stored, most of it just for the pleasure of having a fire.

In addition to insulation, these enormous bales also serve as structure, and are calculated to support the two-story house plus 4 meters (more than 12 feet) of snow. The weight of this much snow, known as a "live load," means that architects must design for an additional 650 kilograms per square meter (that's an extra 135 pounds per square foot). Urs and Christiane had no problem trusting jumbo bales to support the roof over their heads. Laboratory tests had concluded that each bale had a weight-bearing capacity of 32 tons!

On the steeply sloping building site, concrete piers were selected for the foundation. The sturdy columns elevate the structure well above the ground, in anticipation of tall drifts of snow. They also reduce the need for retaining walls and limit the impact of the foundation on the landscape. This foundation supports a concrete slab sub-floor, which is also insulated with jumbo straw bales. To eliminate moisture

▲●■ **ABOVE TOP:** Jumbo bales have five strong strings. Custom bales are created by tying new strings to form a bale of the desired size, then cutting the original strings.

**ABOVE BOTTOM:** Prefabricated wooden door and window frames are lowered into place with a crane, and so are the jumbo bales.

**ABOVE RIGHT:** Jumbo bales have survived lab tests with loads of forty metric tons per bale. In American terms, that's about 2,617 pounds per square foot! (Photograph by Werner Schmidt.)

**FACING BELOW:** A coat of durable lime plaster protects the bales inside and out, and seals them against cold air infiltration. (Photograph by Werner Schmidt.)

transference from the concrete slab, the bales rest on two inches (5 centimeters) of gravel, with a layer of roofing felt as a capillary break. The concrete sub-floor also has drainage holes to allow airflow to evaporate any moisture that might form within the insulation space.

The five-string jumbo bales were lifted onto the building platform with a construction crane and guided into place by a novice crew. Three

courses of bales created 9-foot-high walls for
the first floor; then a wooden "ring beam" was
laid atop the bale walls, which supports the
intermediate ceiling and floor. Werner's crew
stacked another three courses of bales for the
second floor and another beam around the top
of the walls, attaching the roof structure to that.

The walls were finished with four thin coats
of lime plaster, inside and out, totaling about

**RIGHT:** The Brauns spend part of each week in Zurich or Bern for work, and usually three days a week in Disentis. They ski and paraglide. Now they have a young son, Yarl.

**FACING:** The simple contemporary design doesn't compete with the spectacular view.

4 centimeters (1.5 inches). The plaster was sprayed on, then trowelled to a smooth finish. To help bear the weight of the snow, a layer of wire mesh was wrapped around the outside of the strawbale walls, and a poly-mesh was embedded into the final coat of plaster. Says Werner, "I'm very proud that after six years there are no cracks in the plaster."

Urs and Christiane call the house "Refugium Tscheppa," which refers to a child's building block. The idea and message of the home is simplicity—Urs had originally wanted a minimal "hut" for a writer's retreat. Like many ideas, the project grew in scope. And with the location in the Swiss Alps,

good insulation was a primary requirement. After considering Styrofoam, then cardboard bales, he liked Werner's suggestion of straw bales. The simple energy-efficient methodology appealed to Urs, who wanted to build with minimal electronics and technical systems, preferring "things that don't need repair."

He and Christiane also chose a simple, contemporary architectural style, with their spectacular view of the Alps as a focal point. Says Werner, who likes to experiment with building shapes, "With straw bales you can build lots of different forms. If you like a box, you can do that too."

A journey
of a thousand miles
# begins with
## the first step.
—Confucius

## An Inspired Future

Perhaps it is human nature not to change until forced to. Business as usual, habit, and a certain tunnel vision on our individual comforts keep us frogs in the pot, while the water temperature is rising.

But as glaciers melt and oil supplies dwindle, it seems inevitable that global civilizations must recognize the need to transition to some kind of "post-petroleum" future. There is danger here, certainly—and great opportunity. If changes are coming anyway, what if we became proactive and started changing now?

That's precisely what this book intends to inspire: creative choices to meet human housing needs with a lot less energy consumption. The families profiled in this book show that people *can* thrive while reducing demands on our planetary support system.

Imagine if all new construction employed passive solar design combined with super-insulation. What if existing homes added insulation and plugged their air leaks? We could, potentially, reduce our heating and cooling needs to near zero. Sensible, isn't it?

At some point, solar, wind, and other renewable technologies will be able to produce enough energy, right in the neighborhood, to power the good life that all are seeking. There will be less and less need to blow up mountaintops for coal or risk radioactive contamination with expensive nuclear generation. But a hybrid house is just a beginning.

To create truly sustainable societies, we need a shift in awareness. We need to recognize the value in irreplaceable natural systems and our interdependence with the other living creatures on the planet. Our world still has abundant natural resources, which if conservatively managed rather than rapidly exploited, can meet human needs indefinitely.

It has been calculated that if we tried to house the entire world's population with modern manufactured building materials and technologies, it would take the resources of ten planets like Earth. As we make choices each day that reduce demand on oil, steel, concrete, or simply water, we make a difference. If we harvest our trees and mine our mountains more selectively, then salvaging and recycling will become cost

effective and job producing. And we will be preserving something priceless.

What if for every new building that was built, you had to tear down an old one and reuse it? What if we replaced some energy-intensive factory jobs manufacturing products with more jobs on an eco-building site or managing food-producing landscapes? This could work, both economically and socially, because labor is also a renewable resource.

William McDonough wrote in *Cradle To Cradle*, "One of the wonders of human nature is our ability to hope . . . [and] our capacity for acting on our hopes. We not only dream, we strive to achieve the dreams we imagine." He takes inspiration from the four-thousand-year-old tradition of Chinese agriculture, which sustained itself and a thriving culture because of its mutually beneficial relationship with the biological world.

The critical challenge we humans currently face is once again achieving this kind of sustainable balance with nature. If we don't, dire scenarios will likely unfold. If we do, not only will our environment improve, but

there will be less reason for wars, conflicts, and stress at all levels.

My hopes and dreams are of humans reintegrating our endeavors into the regenerative cycles of this living planet and, in the process, creating for ourselves a global Garden of Eden. As Mahatma Ghandi said, "We must be the change that we wish to see in the world." Through our individual intentions and choices, we can each be part of the solution.

# Resources

For additional photographs, information and resources visit: www.HybridHouse.com

## Recommended reading and viewing

There are a plethora of useful and inspiring books, publications, and media available. This short list is just a beginning.

### Books

Baker-Laporte, Paula, Erica Elliott, and John Banta. *Prescriptions for a Healthy House: A Practical Guide for Architects, Builders & Homeowners.* Gabriola Island, British Columbia: New Society Publishers, 2008.

An in-depth guide through the construction process of building a toxin-free home.

Chiras, Dan. *The Homeowner's Guide to Renewable Energy: Achieving Energy Independence from Wind, Solar, Biomass and Hydropower.* Gabriola Island, British Columbia: New Society Publishers, 2006.

Practical energy-saving options available to homeowners retrofitting existing homes.

King, Bruce. *Design of Straw Bale Buildings: The State of the Art.* San Rafael, California: Green Building Press, 2006

Current accumulated laboratory and field experience, interpreted by a host of expert engineers, architects, builders, and building scientists.

Lancaster, Brad. *Rainwater Harvesting for Drylands and Beyond, Vol. 1, 2, 3.* Tucson, Arizona: RainSource Press, 2006, 2008, 2009.

www.HarvestingRainwater.com

A wealth of practical ideas for designing and implementing water-harvesting systems for home, landscape, and community.

Ludwig, Art. *Create An Oasis with Greywater: Choosing, Building and Using Greywater Systems.* Santa Barbara, California: Oasis Press, 2009. www.oasisdesign.com

Twenty different systems demonstrate how to distribute up to half of your household "waste" water into the creation of a lush landscape.

Magwood, Chris, Peter Mack, and Tina Therrien. *More Straw Bale Building: A Complete Guide to Planning and Building with Straw.* Gabriola Island, British Columbia: New Society Publishers, 2005.

A step-by-step guide to strawbale construction, including: permitting, budgeting, designing, drawing up plans, shopping for materials, etc.

Prelitz, Chris. *Green Made Easy: The Everyday Guide for Transitioning to a Green Lifestyle.* Carlsbad, California: Hay House, Inc., 2009.

An inspiring resource of small steps toward sustainability, offering healthful, energy-saving, and money-saving choices for a low-carbon lifestyle.

Steen, Athena, Bill Steen, and Wayne Bingham. *Small Strawbale.* Salt Lake City: Gibbs Smith, Publisher, 2005.

Colorful cottages, sheds, guesthouses, and tiny dwellings present opportunities for experimentation and keeping the ecological footprint modest.

Steinfeld, Carol and David Del Porto. *Reusing the Resource: Adventures in Ecological Wastewater Recycling.* Gabriola Island, British Columbia: New Society Publishers, 2007.

A practical guide to using plants to stabilize, clean, filter, and reuse wastewater while eliminating expensive and polluting sewers and septic tanks.

Venolia, Carol and Kelly Lerner. *Natural Remodeling for the Not-So-Green House: Bringing Your Home into Harmony with Nature.* New York: Lark Books, 2006.

Eco-friendly renovations showcase ideas for greening an existing home in any climate.

Wanek, Catherine. *The New Strawbale Home.* Salt Lake City: Gibbs Smith, Publisher, 2003, 2009.

Floor plans and color photographs of forty strawbale houses across the U.S. and Canada. Includes an overview of strawbale building design essentials.

Weissman, Adam and Katy Bryce, *Using Natural Finishes: A Step-by-Step Guide.* Devon, England: Green Books LTD, 2008.

Design for and application of lime- and earth-based plasters and paints on a variety of traditional and modern wall surfaces. Thorough and beautifully illustrated.

Wilson, Alex and Mark Piepkorn. *Green Building Products: The GreenSpec Guide to Residential Building Materials.* Gabriola Island, British Columbia: BuildingGreen and New Society Publishers, 2008.

Descriptions and manufacturer contacts for more than 1,600 environmentally preferable products.

## DVDs

### Building With Awareness: The Construction of a Hybrid Home

Ted Owens, Syncronos Design, www.buildingwithawareness.com

Artistic and detailed, showing the complete process of building a sustainable home with straw-bale and adobe walls, solar panels, and rainwater harvesting.

# Human Resources: Designers, Builders, Organizations, Networks

## Architects and Designers

### Arkin-Tilt Architects
David Arkin, Anni Tilt
Berkeley, California
510.528.9830
www.arkintilt.com

### Baker-Laporte & Associates
Paula Baker-Laporte
Tesuque, New Mexico
505.989.1813
www.bakerlaporte.com
www.econest.com

### Daniel Matthew Silvernail, Architect
Soquel, California
831.462.9138
www.silvernailarch.com

### Daniel Smith and Associates
Daniel Smith, Dietmar Lorenz
Berkeley, California
510.526.1935
www.dsaarch.com

### Greenweaver, Inc.
Laura Bartels
Carbondale, Colorado
970.379.6779
www.greenweaverinc.com

### Helicon Works
Bill Hutchins, Architect
Takoma Park, Maryland
www.heliconworks.com

### One World Design
Kelly Lerner, Architect
Spokane, WA
509.838.8812
www.one-world-design.com

### San Luis Sustainability Group
Ken Haggard, Polly Cooper & Scott Clark, Architects
Santa Margarita, California
805.438.4452
www.slosustainability.com

## Builders and Engineers

### Boa Constructor Building & Design
Michele Landegger, Debrae Lopes
Watsonville, California
408.848.1117
www.buildingnaturally.com

### HavenCraft Natural Homes
Patrick Marcotte and Sherri Smith
Bancroft, Ontario, Canada
613.332.5872
www.havencraftnaturalhomes.com

### Semmes & Co. Builders, Inc.
Turko Semmes
Atascadero, California
805.466.6737
www.semmesco.com

### Skyhawk Construction
Paul Koppana
Crestone, Colorado
719.256.4505
paulkoppana@hotmail.com

### Sustainable Building Systems
Bob Bolles
Poway, California
Phone: 858.486.6949
www.strawbalehouse.com

### Thangmaker Construction
Frank Meyer
Austin, Texas
512.517.9272
www.thangmaker.com

### Upstate Woodworking, Inc.
David Vail
Rochester, New York
585.292.5697
www.strawbalesystems.com

### Vital Systems—General Contractor
Tim Owen-Kennedy
Ukiah, California
888.859.6336
www.vitalsystems.net

## Organizations and Networks

### Architects, Designers and Planners for Social Responsibility (ADPSR)
Northern California Chapter
http://adpsr-norcal.org/

### Blue Heron Natural Builders Guild
Madison, Wisconsin
www.naturalbuildersguild.com

### Building Engineering Group
Waterloo, Canada
www.civil.uwaterloo.ca/beg

### California Straw Building Association (CASBA)
www.strawbuilding.org

### The Canelo Project
www.caneloproject.com

### Colorado Straw Bale Association (COSBA)
www.coloradostrawbale.org

### The Ecological Building Network (EBNet)
www.ecobuildnetwork.org

### Natural Builders Northeast
www.nbne.org

### The Northwest EcoBuilding Guild
www.ecobuilding.org

**Ontario Straw Bale Building Coalition** (Canada)
www.osbbc.ca

**Solar Energy International (SEI)**
www.solarenergy.org

**Solar Living Institute**
Hopland, California
www.solarliving.org

## European Resources

**amazonnails (England)**
www.strawbalefutures.org.uk

**Architekturbüro/studio di architettura**
Dr. Arch. Margareta Schwarz
Meran, Italy
(0)473/230023
www.archschwarz.com

**Atelier Werner Schmidt**
Werner Schmidt
Trun, Switzerland
+41 (0)81 9432528
www.atelierwernerschmidt.ch

**Austrian StrawBale Network (ASBN) Incl. Austria, Czech Republic, Slovakia, Slovenia, Hungary, Germany**
www.baubiologie.at

**Bauatelier Schmelz & Partner**
Architect Winfried Schmelz
Winklgasse, Austria
+43 (0)2715/2675-0
www.bauatelier.at

**Dutch Straw Bale Association**
www.strobouw.nl

**European eco-building discussion list (mostly in English)**
http://amper.ped.muni.cz/
mailman/listinfo/strawbale

**French Straw-bale Forum**
http://compaillons.naturalforum.net

**German Strawbale Association (FASBA)**
www.fasba.de

**The Passivhaus Institut**
Darmstadt, Germany
www.passivehouse.com

**The Spanish Strawbale Network (Spain)**
www.casasdepaja.org

## Internet Resources

In addition to the online resources mentioned in the body of the book, here are a few trusted websites. Of course, there are countless more. Be sure to get information from a variety of sources and compare.

**BuildingGreen, LLC**
www.buildinggreen.com
Independent, unbiased information on green design and construction materials. A leading professional's source for green products and information. Publishers of *Environmental Building News.*

**Building Science.com**
www.buildingscience.com
Objective, scientific information, promoting the design and construction of buildings that durable, healthy, sustainable and economical.

**CREST Online Discussion Groups**
http://listserv.repp.org/mailman/listinfo/
Lively online dialogues on topics of greenbuilding, strawbale construction, etc., with archives of previous discussions.

**Geiger Research Institute of Sustainable Building**
www.grisb.org

Online collection of sustainable building and appropriate technology resources, including articles, home plans and building codes.

**Healthy Building Network**
www.healthybuilding.net
Updated news about construction materials and health from an authoritative source.

**Hybrid House Network**
www.hybridhouse.com
More photographs, resources, and updated information from the author of this book.

**The Last Straw Journal**
www.thelaststraw.org
Huge online source of U.S. and international resources and information about strawbale and natural building.

**Natural Homes**
www.naturalhomes.org
An amazing interactive map of natural homes around the world, with many links and resources.

**New Leaf America**
www.newleafamerica.com
Online inspiration and step-by-step information about efficiency products and services to assist in a national campaign to retrofit American homes for improved efficiency.

**Sustainable Sources**
www.greenbuilder.com
One of the largest (and oldest) online catalogs of green building resources. Includes a professionals directory, events calendar, and strawbale home registry.